Animals and the Environment

by Jennifer Boothroyd

first step nonfiction

Lerner Publications Company · Minneapolis

Animals need
the **environment.**

Animals use land and water.

Snakes hide under rocks.

Prairie dogs live
under the ground.

Fish live in water.

Animals drink water.

Animals use other animals and plants.

Owls eat small **rodents.**

Monkeys clean each other.

Cows eat grass.

Rabbits hide in the grass.

Animals **adapt** to their environment.

Giraffes have long necks to reach leaves in tall trees.

Lions have **sharp** teeth
to eat meat.

Birds fly to warmer places
in the winter.

Animals use the environment in many ways.

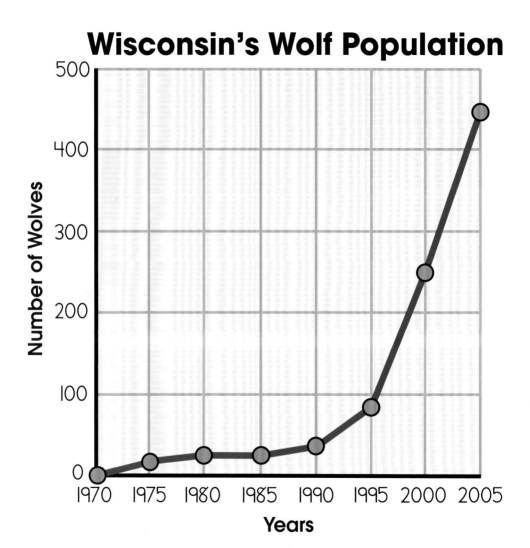

Wisconsin's Wolf Population

Source: U.S. Fish and Wildlife Service

The Gray Wolf Returns

Long ago, thousands of wolves lived in Wisconsin. People began hunting the wolves. Soon there were fewer wolves. Their population became smaller. In the late 1960s, the government decided that people could no longer hunt wolves in Wisconsin. Look at the chart on page 18. What happened to Wisconsin's wolf population after 1970, when people stopped hunting wolves?

Animal Facts

 Scientists have discovered over one million different plants and animals. Most scientists believe there are millions that haven't been discovered yet.

 Many animals have become extinct in the last one hundred years. Extinct means those animals have died out. None of those animals are left in the world.

 More than 400 birds, animals, and fish in the United States are endangered. Endangered means the animal is likely to become extinct.

 Some animals are helpful to humans. A brown bat can eat 600 mosquitoes in one hour.

 Some animals make problems for humans. Beavers cut down trees to make their homes in rivers. Their homes block rivers and can cause small floods.

Glossary

 adapt – change

 environment – the land, water, air, weather, and living things of the earth

 rodents – animals, such as mice and rats, that have large front teeth for gnawing

 sharp – able to cut or tear

Index

The images in this book are used with the permission of: © John R. Kreul/Independent Picture Service, pp. 2, 22 (second from top); PhotoDisc Royalty Free by Getty Images, pp. 3, 5, 6, 7, 8, 13, 14, 17, 22 (top); © Joe McDonald/Visuals Unlimited, p. 4; © Michael Quinton, pp. 9, 22 (bottom); © Jonathan & Angela/Taxi/Getty Images, p. 10; Agricultural Research Service, USDA, p. 11; © Leonard Lee Rue III, p. 12; © Royalty-Free/CORBIS, pp. 15, 22 (second from bottom); © David W Hamilton/The Image Bank/Getty Images, p. 16; U.S. Fish and Wildlife Service, p. 18.

Front cover: PhotoDisc Royalty Free by Getty Images

Lerner Publications Company
A division of Lerner Publishing Group, Inc.
241 First Avenue North
Minneapolis, MN 55401 U.S.A.

Website address: www.lernerbooks.com

Library of Congress Cataloging-in-Publication Data

Boothroyd, Jennifer, 1972-
    Animals and the environment / by Jennifer Boothroyd.
        p.   cm. — (First step nonfiction. Ecology)
    Includes index.
    ISBN 978-0-8225-8602-9 (lib. bdg. : alk. paper)
    ISBN 978-0-7613-3990-8 (eBook)
    1. Animal ecology—Juvenile literature.
    I. Title.
    QH541.14.B66 2008
    591.7—dc22   2007007809

Manufactured in the United States of America
3 – PC – 3/1/13